THE **CHANGING RAILWAY** SCENE

Western Region

LAURENCE WATERS

Ian Allan
PUBLISHING

First published 2008

ISBN 978 0 7110 3275 0

Published by Ian Allan Publishing Ltd, Hersham, Surrey KT12 4RG.
Printed in England by Ian Allan Printing Ltd, Hersham, Surrey KT12 4RG.

Code: 0809/C1

Visit the Ian Allan Publishing website at:
www.ianallanpublishing.com

Below: Class 52 'Western' diesel-hydraulic No 1023 *Western Fusilier* heads the 11-coach 09.00 Paignton–Newcastle service through Dawlish on 20 September 1975. Withdrawn in February 1977, this locomotive is nowadays preserved at the National Railway Museum, York.
P. A. Fry/Great Western Trust

Contents

Introduction   6

1   The 'Great Western' Region   22

2   Branch and Secondary-Line Services   30

3   Freights   38

4   Steam Depots   42

5   Swindon Works   46

6   Regional Boundary Changes   48

7   Diesel Multiple-Units   58

8   Diesel-Hydraulics   66

9   The Diesel-Electric Era   78

10 Swindon Finale   94

11 Last Years of the Western Region   95

Introduction

The Nationalisation of Britain's railways on 1 January 1948 brought together not just the 'Big Four' main line companies, but also 50 or so smaller companies into a new, government-controlled British Railways.

Of the six new regions that were formed under the 1947 Transport Act it was the Western Region more than the other five that probably changed the least from the previous company. This was most obviously due to the retention of the Great Western locomotive numbering scheme, as well of course to the thousands of staff who were still working essentially for the Great Western Railway in everything but name.

The newly formed Western Region inherited some 3,742 route miles of track, hundreds of stations, nearly 4,000 steam and diesel locomotives, 130 locomotive depots and sub sheds, and a large amount of coaching and freight rolling stock, much of which had seen better days. The Second World War, together with the slow post-war recovery, resulted in large parts of the railway infrastructure being left in a run down condition. Investment was needed, but the years after Nationalisation brought little real investment, with the railways being under-funded by successive governments.

This slowed down any form of real modernisation, and it was not until the 1955 Modernisation Plan that a positive start was made in addressing this problem. The plan set out to produce 'a thoroughly modern system' and to exploit the great national advantages of railways as bulk transporters of passengers and goods. It was estimated that the time required to implement the plan nationwide would be 15 years, at an estimated cost of £1,240 million; a lot of money in 1955. The plan included the replacement of steam locomotives with diesel and electric traction, new passenger rolling stock, a complete remodelling of freight services and importantly, track and signalling improvements.

The 1955 plan at last provided much-needed finance for some infrastructure investment on the Western Region. New schemes included the provision of additional carriage sidings and servicing facilities, at Goodrington near Paignton, which were opened in June 1957, and an automated marshalling yard at Margam, near Port Talbot, which was opened in 1960.

In 1958, £1.8 million was made available by the British Transport Commission for improvements at Plymouth, with the provision of multiple aspect signalling (MAS), and the completion of the rebuilding of Plymouth North Road station. The new station at Plymouth, which had been partially reconstructed by the Great Western in 1939 before work was abandoned due to the Second World War, was opened on 26 March 1962 by the then chairman of the British Railways Board, Dr Richard Beeching.

The other main work undertaken at this time was the provision of a new station and track layout at Banbury, with the work being completed during 1958.

One of the biggest investments on the Western Region at this time was on re-signalling the system. With money available, a start was made in converting the region's main lines from semaphore to multiple aspect signalling (colour light), and at the same time opening a number of large power signalboxes, each one covering a wide area. The new power boxes, replaced hundreds of manual boxes over the system, with a saving in maintenance, and probably more importantly, in labour costs.

During 1961, a start was made on re-signalling the Paddington area, and on 8 October 1962 the Western Region opened a new power box at Old Oak Common. The scheme was extended to cover the 25-mile section between Hayes and Reading, which was completed with the opening on 13 October 1963, of a new power box at Slough. MAS was extended to Reading and beyond with the opening of a new power box at Reading on 26 April 1965, which controlled 64 route miles, and replaced 42 manual boxes. Sadly, with the introduction of MAS, and the subsequent outsourcing in the manufacture of equipment, the old Great Western signal works at Caversham Road, Reading, opened by the GWR in around 1859, became redundant, and was closed on 29 June 1984.

As the re-signalling spread, new electronic (power) boxes were opened at Birmingham Snow Hill, Bristol, Cardiff, Newport, Port Talbot, Swindon, and Westbury.

The Bristol scheme was the largest on the region costing some £4 million. It covered 114 route miles and resulted in the closure of 70 manual boxes. By 1984, over 800 route miles had been converted to MAS.

Another significant change took place with introduction by British Rail during 1974 of the nationwide Total Operations Processing System (TOPS). This computerised system saw all locomotives renumbered into various power and sub classes. The system allowed a central control to track not only all motive power, but also coaches and wagons on a day-to-day basis.

The introduction of the 125mph HSTs in 1976/77 saw a considerable amount of track reconstruction and signal modifications on the ex-Great Western main line, both along the Thames Valley to Bristol and South Wales, and later, from Reading to Taunton and Plymouth. On the safety side, the Western inherited the GWR-designed automatic train control system (ATC). This was an excellent system that had proved itself over many years of use, and continued to give good service on the Western Region. Unfortunately, ATC was not adopted by the other regions, and was eventually replaced by the BR-designed automatic train warning system (AWS). However, it was not until 1972/73 that the changeover from ATC to AWS was completed on the Western Region.

For a number of years after Nationalisation, the Western Region was essentially still operating its services over the old Great Western system. This changed on 1 February 1958 with the first of a number of regional boundary alterations. From this date the Western Region took control of the Somerset & Dorset line between Bath and Templecombe, and also the ex-Midland Railway route from Bristol to Birmingham as far as Barnt Green. The Western also lost some territory as on the same date control of the Weymouth area passed to the Southern Region, and within a few years, Waterloo not Paddington, became the departure station for main line services to Weymouth.

Under Western Region control, steam motive power over the S&D and the Midland route from Bristol to Birmingham remained relatively unchanged, although a few ex-Great Western locomotives were allocated to both Bath and Templecombe sheds. Also during the same year, the ex-Great Western & Great Central Joint line to Marylebone became part of the Eastern Region.

Further and more widespread changes took place on 1 January 1963, which resulted in Western Region lines in North Wales and the Midlands being transferred to the London Midland Region. This was offset to some degree with the transfer of Southern Region lines West of Salisbury, together with the southern half of the Somerset & Dorset into Western Region control. From the operating perspective, apart from a few ex-GWR types, the motive power stayed essentially the same on these lines. The main services via the LSWR route to Exeter and Plymouth were still being operated using Southern Bulleid Pacifics, and on the Bristol to Birmingham line ex-LMS 'Jubilee' and Class 5 4-6-0s continued to provide the bulk of the motive power. It was an interesting situation with the Western suddenly

Below: **Ex-Great Western 'Castle' 4-6-0 No 5070 *Sir Daniel Gooch* from Old Oak Common (81A) passes Fairwood Junction signalbox near Westbury on 8 June 1963 with the 10.10am relief service from Torquay to Paddington. This was the last year of regular 'Castle' haulage to and from the South West. No 5070 was withdrawn in March 1964. The opening of a new powerbox at Westbury on 13 May 1984 resulted in the closure of Fairwood Junction signalbox and also 12 other boxes in the area.** *P. A. Fry/Great Western Trust*

Above: **A typical Western Region branch train of the 1950s and early 1960s seen here at Brecon as ex-Great Western '5700' class 0-6-0PT arrives with a morning service from Newport on 26 November 1962. The Beeching cuts of the 1960s saw many of these branch lines closed, the Newport to Brecon passenger service being withdrawn on 31 December 1962.** *Charles Gordon-Stuart/Great Western Trust*

acquiring ex-Southern and LMS locomotives into its book stock, and the Midland in particular acquiring a large number of former Great Western locomotives. However, under a maintenance agreement, repairs of ex-GW locomotives were still undertaken at Swindon. Whilst Derby and Crewe continued to repair the ex-LMS locomotives, ex-Southern locomotives were repaired at Eastleigh.

In May 1961, Sir Brian Robertson retired as chairman of the British Transport Commission and was replaced by Dr Richard Beeching. The Beeching report into the state of the railways in this country was published in 1962, and the widespread closures that followed the report had a profound effect on the Western Region. Although the region had closed some uneconomic lines in the years prior to the report, the Beeching cuts of the 1960s saw counties such as Devon, Gloucestershire, Oxfordshire, Somerset, and Wiltshire lose most, and in some cases all, of their branch line services. The large number of line closures during the 1960s and 1970s, together with the regional boundary changes, reduced the Western Region to about half of its size at Nationalisation. By 1980, the route mileage of the WR had dropped to 1,903 miles, serving 493 stations and depots.

During the 1970s and 1980s, the use of the private car was having quite an effect on passenger numbers, and to address this problem the Western introduced a number of Parkway stations. These were either completely new or revamped existing stations, each provided with large car parks. The first to be opened was Bristol Parkway, the new station being situated on the site of Stoke Gifford yard on the South Wales main line just north of Bristol, and was opened on 1 May 1972. This was followed by Bodmin Parkway on 1 November 1983, Port Talbot Parkway on 3 December 1984, Didcot Parkway on 19 June 1985, and Tiverton Parkway on 12 May 1986. Car owners were initially tempted with free parking, but this did not last for long. The 1980s also saw the opening of three new stations in South Wales, at Cardiff Cathays on 3 October 1983, Cwmbran on 12 May 1985, and Lisvane & Thornhill on 4 November 1985.

On 16 May 1983, a new station was opened at Pinhoe on the ex-LSWR main line east of Exeter, and also in the South West, a new station was opened on the St Ives branch at Lelant Saltings as part of the St Ives park-and-ride scheme. The Thingley Junction to Trowbridge line was closed to passengers on 18 April 1966, but on 13 May 1985, a limited passenger service was introduced between Swindon and Melksham.

The end of the Western Region as we knew it, came on 10 June 1986, when the five regions were abolished, and replaced by new business sectors such as InterCity,

Network SouthEast, Regional Railways and Railfreight. Each of these new sectors had its own corporate livery, which resulted in the end of the BR blue livery period.

The changing motive power

In the years after Nationalisation, the Western Region continued to operate its services using motive power, much of which dated from before the Second World War. The lack of immediate replacements saw some ex-Great Western designs still being constructed well into the 1950s. The introduction of the various BR Standard types during 1951 did little to ease the ageing Western Region fleet. 'Castle' class 4-6-0s that had been designed by Collett in 1923 were still being constructed some two years after Nationalisation, with the last of the class, No 7037 *Swindon* being turned out in August 1950. Other 4-6-0 types such as 'Modified Halls' and 'Manors' continued in production until October and December 1950 respectively. These were fine designs, and were needed to replace the ageing 'Star' and 'Saint' class 4-6-0s, both of which were designed before the First World War. Between 1952 and 1953 Swindon also constructed a number of LMS Ivatt-designed 2MT 2-6-0s, primarily for use on the Cambrian lines in North Wales.

Construction of smaller tank classes such as the '1600' and '9400' class 0-6-0PTs continued even longer, the last '1600' class, No 1669 being completed at Swindon in May 1955, and the last '9400' class, No 3409, in October 1956. However, it is worth remembering that apart from the first ten of the '9400s', which comprised 200 locomotives, they were all built for the Western Region by outside contractors, and not at Swindon Works. These were needed to replace many of the older 0-6-0PTs, but one wonders why these were not replaced from the start by the new BR 0-6-0 (later Class 08) diesel shunters. These were built initially at Derby and

were introduced by BR in October 1952, with the Western Region taking delivery of the first five from new, and by December 1953 the Western was operating 20 of the first 40 to be built.

Although ordered by the Great Western Railway, it was the Western Region that took delivery of two experimental gas turbine locomotives. The first of these was No 18000, which was soon given the nickname 'Kerosene Castle', arrived in May 1950, and No 18100 in December 1951. Neither was particularly successful, and both were soon withdrawn in 1960 and 1958 respectively.

During 1953, the last few examples of the 'Saint' class 4-6-0s were withdrawn from service, the last one, No 2920 *St David*, built at Swindon in 1907,was the subject of a failed preservation attempt, and was withdrawn in October 1953. The remaining 'Star' class 4-6-0s lasted until 1957, the final one, No 4056 *Princess Margaret*, built at Swindon in 1914, was withdrawn in October 1957.

The first of the new BR Standard types, the 'Britannia' class 4-6-2s, were delivered to the Western Region during 1952.The first ten, Nos 70015 to 70024 were initially allocated to Old Oak Common, and Plymouth Laira, and put to work on services to and from the South West. A further five, Nos 70025 to 70029 were allocated from new to Cardiff Canton. The 'Britannias' were not popular with the South West crews, and within a few years all 15 Western Region examples were working

Below: **Even with the introduction of diesel multiple-units, the Western Region was still operating ex-Great Western push-pull services on a number of lines well into the 1960s. Pictured here arriving at Tiverton with the 10.45am service from Exeter St Davids to Dulverton on 1 September 1962 is ex-Great Western 0-4-2T No 1466. Many of these branch lines were closed under the Beeching cuts of the early 1960s. The Exeter to Dulverton branch closed to passengers on 7 October 1963. No. 1466 has been preserved and can be seen at Didcot Railway Centre.** *P.A. Fry /Great Western Trust*

from Cardiff Canton. Here, they were used with great success on fast services to London, and over the North & West route to Shrewsbury. Interestingly, this was the first time that a Pacific type had worked on regular passenger services over GW metals since the Great Western's *Great Bear*, which was built in 1908 and withdrawn in 1924.

Apart from the GWR-designed 0-6-0PTs, between 1951 and 1960, Swindon also constructed a large number of BR Standard types, many for the other regions. Construction comprised 80 Class 4 4-6-0s, 20 Class 3 2-6-0s, 45 Class 3 2-6-2Ts and 54 Class 9F 2-10-0s. Between 1952 and 1965 the Western Region operated six different classes of BR Standard locomotives.

The Great Western had designed its locomotives specifically to operate each type of service, both reliably and efficiently, 'horses for courses' so to speak, and this is one reason why the Western Region continued to construct the older designs well after Nationalisation. It is probably true to say that apart from the '9F' 2-10-0s, none of the other BR Standard class locomotives performed any better on Western Region services than the older, ex-Great Western designs.

During the 1950s and early 1960s, WR main line passenger services were in the hands of 'King', and 'Castle' class 4-6-0s. The 'Kings' were generally used on the heaviest trains, with the 'Castles' on some of the fastest. Although both classes were good performers, they had their performance improved with the fitting of double blastpipes and chimneys, and four-row super-heaters. All 30 'Kings' were modified between 1956 and 1958, and some 66 Castles, between 1958 and 1961. The bulk of the rest of the passenger and fast freight services were handled by the mixed traffic 'Counties', 'Halls', 'Granges' and 'Manor' class 4-6-0s. Churchward's rather elderly Class 4300 2-6-0s were still good locomotives, being used on both passenger and freight. Secondary services (freight and passenger), were mainly operated using a variety of 2-6-2T, 0-6-2T, 0-6-0PT, and 0-4-2T classes. Churchward's large '4700' class 2-8-0s could still be seen on fast fitted freights, and weekend passenger relief services, right up until the early 1960s.

Heavy and long-distance freight services were still being operated with the Churchward '2800' and Collett '2884'class 2-8-0s, supplemented by Collett's '7200' class 2-8-2Ts, and also ex-War Department (WD) 2-8-0s, and Stanier-designed but Swindon-built LMS Class 8F 2-8-0s.

The main locomotive and carriage works on the Western Region was situated at Swindon, with smaller works at Newton Abbot, Worcester, Wolverhampton Stafford Road, Barry, and Caerphilly. Most of the larger

steam depots also had their own lifting shops. In 1957 the Western Region was operating a fleet of around 3,500 steam locomotives, which were allocated between nine motive power districts, comprising a total of 62 main steam sheds and 63 sub sheds.

On 23 June 1962, the Great Western Railway Museum was opened at Swindon. Situated in an old railway chapel, it initially housed the replica broad gauge 2-2-2 *North Star* that for many years had stood on display in Swindon Works 'A' shop. Other locomotives in the museum included 'Star' class 4-6-0 No 4003 *Lode Star*, Dean Goods 0-6-0 No 2516, '9400' class 0-6-0PT No 9400, and 4-4-0 No 3440 *City of Truro*, which had been taken out of service on 17 May 1961 following restoration to the main line in 1957.

The biggest change in Western motive power came between 1958 and 1964, first with the introduction of diesel-hydraulic locomotives and diesel multiple units (DMUs), and from 1963, with diesel-electrics.

The first hydraulic locomotives to be introduced were the five North British-built 'Warship' Type 4 (later Class 41), AIA-AIAs that were delivered during 1958. On 22 August, No D601 *Ark Royal* powered the first diesel-hauled 'Cornish Riviera Express' between Penzance and Paddington. Although these first five 'Warships' were not the most reliable of locomotives they paved the way for the introduction of the Swindon and North British type 4, B-B (Class 42 and 43) 'Warships'. These were also introduced during 1958/59, and after testing, were put to work on services to and from the South West.

The North British B-B Type 2s (Class 22) were also introduced during 1959 and were used on secondary passenger and freight services, again initially in the South West. The number of diesel-hydraulic locomotives increased with the delivery in 1961, of the first of the Beyer Peacock B-B Type 3 (Class 35) 'Hymeks', and in 1962, the highly successful Swindon and Crewe-built C-C Type 4 (Class 52) 'Westerns' came into service. The modern overall design of the 'Westerns' was the result of input by the British Railways Design Panel. The last of the diesel-hydraulic types to be delivered was the Swindon-built Type 1 (Class 14) 0-6-0s during 1964, and by this date the Western was operating a total of 365 diesel-hydraulic locomotives.

The introduction of the 'Warships' had displaced a number of 'Castles' and 'Kings' from the South West. Plymouth Laira lost its allocation of 'Kings' in September 1960, but they found new work on services to and from South Wales, and on the one-hourly interval services from Paddington to Birmingham and Wolverhampton. Cardiff Canton gained its very first allocation of 'Kings' in December 1960. Their arrival saw the remaining 'Britannias' transferred to the London Midland Region.

It was the introduction of the Class 35 'Hymeks', and Class 52 'Westerns' that resulted in the decimation of the Western Region's express passenger steam fleet. Withdrawals of 'Castles' had been slow, with only twelve being withdrawn between 1959 and 1961. The introduction of the 'Hymeks' saw them take over many of the old 'Castle' class turns on services to Bristol, South Wales, and later to Worcester, and this led to 57 members of the class being withdrawn during 1962. Interestingly, seven of these had been fitted with four-row superheaters, and double blast pipes and chimneys only a year before. Sadly, during the same year, all 30 members of the 'King' class were withdrawn although many were still in excellent condition, but they were deemed surplus to requirements. The problem with the 'Kings' was their double-red route restriction, which confined them to certain main lines only, which meant that they could not really be used for anything else.

In 1963, with the Class 52 'Westerns' coming into service, a further 47 'Castles' were withdrawn. The rapid run down of steam saw the closure of the ex-Rhymney Railway works at Caerphilly in June 1963, and the ex-Great Western works at Wolverhampton Stafford Road in February 1964. The decision by the Western not to order any more diesel-hydraulics and to switch to diesel-electric power saw the first of the new English Electric Type 3 Co-Cos (later Class 37) delivered in April 1963. These were initially allocated to Newport,

Cardiff and Landore, and they soon took over many of the freight services in South Wales.

These were followed in December 1963 by the new Brush Type 4 Co-Co (later Class 47) diesel-electric locomotives, and within a year members of the class were allocated to Old Oak Common, Bristol Bath Road and Cardiff Canton, Swansea Landore, and even for a short time, to Worcester. The South West became fully dieselised with the withdrawal of all steam working west of Bridgwater during the spring of 1964.

The Class 47s, which became the mainstay of Western Region services long after the hydraulics had gone, were true mixed traffic locomotives, and sounded the death knell for many ex- Great Western types. During 1964, a further 37 'Castles' were withdrawn, and the same withdrawal rate was taking place across the board with the other ex-GWR classes, and by January 1965 the Western Region book stock probably stood at around a total of 200 working steam locomotives.

With dieselisation almost complete, the Western Region took the decision to withdraw all steam services from 31 December 1965. With steam gone the works at Swindon was rationalised with closure of the carriage works and many steam-related buildings.

By the late 1960s, the diesel-hydraulic 'Warships', and the North British Class 22s were becoming unreliable, while another problem was that the latter were soon found to be underpowered. One of the major difficulties with these locomotives was the source of spare parts after the North British Company went into liquidation in 1962. The five D600 series 'Warships' were withdrawn in 1967, and in 1968, the first three of the Swindon-built D800 series 'Warships' were withdrawn, together with a number of the Class 22s.

Mention must be made of the BR Class 14 diesel-hydraulic 0-6-0s. A total of 56 of these locomotives were built at Swindon during 1964/65, just at the time many branch lines were closing. They were designed for

Below: **The 'Warship' class diesel-hydraulics were introduced by the Western Region in 1958 and took over many of the services from the ex-Great Western 'Castle' and 'King' class 4-6-0s. Pictured here arriving at Torquay on a beautiful summer's day in 1959 is Swindon-built No D806** *Cambrian* **with the down 'Torbay Express' – the 12.00noon service from Paddington to Kingswear. The BR Mk1 coaching stock has been painted in chocolate and cream, this livery having been introduced by the Western Region on some main line services during 1956 to reflect the old company.** *Great Western Trust*

shunting and trip working, and with this type of work drying up they soon became redundant. In retrospect, they probably should never have been built, and by 1966 20 members of the class were already in store, and during 1968/69 the whole class was withdrawn. There was nothing really wrong with the type, it was just lack of work, and many were sold to private companies, both at home and abroad, where they continued to give good service for many years.

Derby-built Class 116 diesel multiple-units (DMUs) were introduced on suburban services in the Birmingham area during 1957. The new services ran from Snow Hill and Moor Street to Leamington and Stratford-upon-Avon, and northwards to Wolverhampton, Kidderminster and Wellington. Although initially operated by the Western Region, these services were taken over by the London Midland Region from January 1958.

In South Wales, Class 116 DMUs were also introduced on Cardiff Valley services between Cardiff and Treherbert in September 1957, and were extended to cover all the Valley services in January 1958. During the same year, Swindon built Class 120 three-car 'Cross County' sets which were introduced on services between Bristol, Cardiff and Birmingham. In 1960, Pressed Steel Class 117 DMUs took over many of the suburban services in the Thames Valley, and also secondary services in the South West. In 1962, the London Midland Region introduced Derby-built Class 115s on suburban and intermediate services over the ex-Western Region 'Chiltern Line' between Marylebone, High Wycombe and Banbury.

The servicing of DMUs in the Birmingham area was undertaken at Tyseley, and in South Wales initially at Barry and Cardiff Cathays, and later at Cardiff Canton, where a large, purpose-built servicing facility was constructed in the old carriage sheds. DMU servicing was also undertaken at Plymouth Laira, Bristol St Philip's Marsh, Swansea Landore, and in the London area, at the old steam shed at Southall, which after its closure to steam in 1965, had been converted to a DMU maintenance depot. Southall was closed in 1986 when a new purpose-built facility was opened at Reading. The Chiltern Line DMUs were serviced by the London Midland Region at both Marylebone and Bletchley.

The introduction of diesel-hydraulic locomotives in the South West during 1959 saw the need for proper, purpose-built diesel servicing facilities. This was initially provided at Newton Abbot, where the old steam works was converted to become the Western Region's first diesel maintenance depot. However with more and more hydraulics being delivered, for a few years at least maintenance work and minor running repairs were

Below: **Diesel multiple-units were first used by the Western Region on some South Wales Valley line services in September 1957, and by 1962 DMUs were to be seen on many of the Western Region intermediate services. Pictured here arriving at Aynho (for Deddington) with a Banbury to Oxford stopping service on 14 June 1962 is Pressed Steel (Class 117) three-car suburban unit headed by No W51413. Note the mail van on the back.** *Charles Gordon-Stuart/Great Western Trust*

Above: **The Beyer Peacock B-B Type 3 (Class 35) 'Hymeks' were introduced by the Western Region in 1961, and soon took over many of the 'Castle' class turns on services to both Bristol and South Wales. Pictured here at West Ealing on 1 June 1963 is Hymek No D7066 with a down milk empties to the South West.**
Charles Gordon-Stuart/Great Western Trust

carried out at a number of steam depots. This was an unsatisfactory situation and may well have had some influence on the unreliability of the D600 and D800 series 'Warships' and the D6300 series Class 22s.

The situation was improved when the Western opened further maintenance depots at Plymouth Laira where a new diesel servicing facility was opened at the steam depot in 1960, and at Bristol Bath Road where a new, purpose-built diesel depot was opened in June 1962. These were followed with the opening of Swansea Landore in May 1963, at Newport Ebbw Junction in September 1963, and Cardiff Canton in September 1964. Perhaps surprisingly, even though the Class 52 'Westerns' had been introduced on Paddington–Birmingham services in 1962, a dedicated diesel maintenance depot was not opened at Old Oak Common until October 1965. Prior to this, a stabling and refuelling point was opened in April 1964, at the old steam-servicing yard at Ranelagh Bridge, just outside Paddington. The Western Region's aim of having a completely dieselised service in the South West was not entirely possible due to the poor reliability of the diesel-hydraulics, and steam continued to be seen in the area until April 1964.

Dieselisation on the rest of the Western was relatively slow, with steam still being the main motive power on many lines. Main line passenger services between Paddington and Worcester via Oxford continued to be hauled by 'Castle' class locomotives until 1964, when 'Hymek' Class 35s replaced them. The very last scheduled steam service from Paddington was the 16.15 service to Banbury on 11 June 1965, hauled by No 7029 *Clun Castle*.

On the Cambrian lines in North Wales the London Midland Region continued to use 'Manor' class 4-6-0s on the 'Cambrian Coast Express' right up until the class was withdrawn on 30 November 1965. Steam officially finished on the Western Region on 31 December 1965, however the last main line steam service on the region actually ran on Monday, 3 January when 'Modified Hall' No 6998 *Burton Agnes Hall* pulled the 14.20 service from Oxford to Newcastle, as far as Banbury. Another member of the class, No 6999 *Capel Dewi Hall*, had been on station pilot duty at Oxford the previous day.

It is worth mentioning that for a number of years prior to the end of steam, the Western Region as a whole, had struggled to find steam locomotive servicing and maintenance staff. This meant that the condition of many of the remaining steam locomotives left a lot to be desired. Some years ago the shedmaster at Oxford, the late Joe Trethewey, told me that during the 1960s, Oxford had a continual shortage of shed maintenance staff, due in no small measure to the local BMC car, and Pressed Steel body plants at Cowley, not just paying better wages, but providing a cleaner working environment.

One by one during this period, the old steam locomotive depots, many of which dated from the turn of the century were closed, most completely, but at some, diesel refuelling facilities replaced the old shed buildings. The removal of steam from Western Region services saw diesel locomotive maintenance and repair

work concentrated at just six main depots: Old Oak Common, Bristol Bath Road, Cardiff Canton, Swansea Landore, Newton Abbot and Plymouth Laira.

During 1972, the remaining 'Warships' and the D6300s were withdrawn, leaving little work for the Western's first diesel maintenance depot at Newton Abbot, which was closed. Other diesel-electric locomotives to arrive on the Western at this time were the Brush Type 2s (Class 31s). These came from the Eastern Region, and were used on a number of passenger services over the region including Bristol to Weymouth, Paddington to Worcester, and Paddington to Birmingham services via Oxford. The arrival of the '31s' signalled the end for the Class 35 'Hymeks', and apart from a handful of locomotives that lasted until 1974/75, the majority of the class were withdrawn during 1971/72.

The BR Sulzer Class 25s arrived from the London Midland Region during 1972. These were at first used mainly on freight, but later on secondary passenger services. The Class 25s were initially allocated to Plymouth Laira, Bristol Bath Road and Newport Ebbw Junction, but although they were quite successful, they did not last for long on the Western Region, with the last few examples being either withdrawn or transferred away during October 1980.

The Class 52s kept the hydraulic flag flying well into the 1970s, but the introduction during the summer of 1972 of BR air-braked Mk2 stock on services to and from the South West saw many of them replaced by

Class 47s. The final influx of diesel-electrics came with the introduction of the English Electric Class 50 locomotives on Western Region services during 1974. Electrification of the West Coast main line had made these 2,700hp locomotives redundant. The Class 50s were the first 100mph diesels on the Western Region, and they were used with the new, fully air-conditioned BR Mk2d/e/f stock on services to Bristol and the South West.

Apart from the obvious changes from steam to diesel-hydraulic, and from diesel-hydraulic to diesel-electric traction, arguably the biggest move forward in motive power came with the introduction during 1976 of the InterCity Class 253 High Speed Trains (HSTs). Prior to their introduction, the Western Region operated a prototype Class 252 HST on services between Paddington and Bristol.

On the Western Region, the HSTs were capable of continuous 125mph high-speed running and once established they took over services to South Wales, Bristol and the South West. The displaced Class 50s were then moved to Worcester and Birmingham services. The few remaining 'Western' Class 52s soldiered on, often filling in for failed Class 47s and 50s, and hauling aggregate trains from the Mendip stone terminals. The majority of the class were withdrawn during 1975/76, but the last seven examples survived in service until February 1977.

The withdrawal of the diesel-hydraulics saw the role of Swindon as a major locomotive repair works diminish, with work comprising the repair of '08' diesel shunters, and Western and Southern Region multiple-units. The works became a major location for the storage and subsequent cutting up of withdrawn diesels. Apart from disposing of most of the diesel-hydraulics during the 1960s and '70s, between 1972 and 1985 the works also cut up a total of 410 diesel-electric locomotives, comprising Class 08s, Sulzer Class 25s, English Electric Class 40s, and Crewe and Derby-built 'Peak' Class 45s and 46s. Once this work began to dry up, and with impeccable timing, British Rail Engineering announced in early 1985, that the works would close, the announcement being made just prior to the planned GWR 150 anniversary celebrations. The exhibition, which had been months in planning, was subsequently cancelled.

The works, which had been established by Daniel Gooch in 1843, finally closed in 1986. The site was sold to Tarmac Ltd, and apart from the buildings which now form part of the Great Western retail outlet centre, and the 'Steam' museum, housing and other retail outlets now cover the rest of the site. The old GWR drawing office is now part of the National Monument Record Centre. In its heyday the locomotive and carriage works covered an area of 323 acres of which some 75 acres were under cover, the main locomotive 'A' shop alone covering an area of 11½ acres. Its importance to the town of Swindon can be gained from the fact that in 1901, the Great Western was employing about 12,000 at the works out of a town population of about 45,000.

Passenger services
Western Region passenger services during the first few years after Nationalisation saw little change from the period before. The austerity years after the war had seen the timings on many of the services eased, and this was continued until the early 1950s.
Apart from the short-lived experiment of painting the 'King' class 4-6-0s blue, locomotives were still being turned out after repair in what was essentially Great Western Brunswick green livery.

The livery for passenger coaching stock was, however, standardised across all six regions with the introduction of a British Railways' corporate 'strawberry and cream' colour scheme, and in 1951, the first of the BR Standard Mk1 coaches were introduced. These were soon to be found on many of the Western Region's main line services. The influx of the Mk1s resulted in the rapid withdrawal of many of the ex-Great Western coaches that had pretty much been in constant use since the 1930s.

During the 1950s, slip coach working, although in decline, still formed an important part of Western Region services. In 1955, there were three daily slip coach services at Reading, with coaches being slipped from the 8.30am Plymouth, the 4.5pm Weymouth and the 1.50pm Bristol. This latter service ended on 12 September 1958, the other two having ended several months earlier. Other slip coach services at this time included a multiple detachment at Didcot from the up 7am train from Weston-super-Mare, and a single slip at Bicester from the 5.10pm down fast service to Wolverhampton. As late as 1958, the Western Region had converted three Hawksworth brake composites into slip coaches to replace older, ex-GWR vehicles. The slip workings were a costly option, both in operation and the fact that each coach required its own

Below: **The English Electric Type 4 (later Class 50) arrived from the London Midland Region in 1974, and was initially used on services to the South West of England, using air-conditioned BR Mk 2 stock. During 1978 they were named after Royal Navy warships, many taking the names of withdrawn diesel-hydraulic Class 42s and Class 43s. Here No 50024 *Vanguard* passes the site of Savernake West Junction on 7 April 1980 with the 9.25am service from Penzance to Paddington.**
P. A. Fry/ Great Western Trust

guard, and it was on economic grounds that these services were withdrawn. The final Didcot slip was on 7 June 1960, with the Bicester slip, the last one in the country, on 9 September 1960.

Of the many services, the Paddington to Bristol, and the Paddington to Plymouth, and Penzance service was always important to both the Great Western and the Western Region. The 'flagship' service between Paddington and Bristol was the non-stop 'Bristolian'. In the period before the Second World War the service was timed at 105 minutes in each direction. It was withdrawn during hostilities and was not resurrected until 1951, but it was not until the summer of 1954 that the old timing of 105 minutes was restored. The reintroduced service was initially hauled by 'King' class 4-6-0s, but by 1958 the train was in the hands of 'Castle' class 4-6-0s which had been improved with the fitting of four-row superheaters, double blastpipes and chimneys, and a greatly improved mechanical lubrication system. On 28 April 1958, No 7018 *Drysllwyn Castle* recorded the fastest steam run, covering the 117.6 miles from Bristol to Paddington in just 93 minutes 50 seconds.

The 'Cornish Riviera (Limited) Express' was the most famous train on both the Great Western and the Western

Region. The 10.30am service from Paddington to Penzance had been introduced before the First World War. In the 1950s, the service was hauled by a 'King' through to Plymouth. On summer Saturdays, apart from a brief stop at Newton Abbot to attach a pilot locomotive, and another locomotive change at Plymouth, the run was essentially non-stop right through to Truro, reaching Penzance in 6 hours 40 minutes.

The introduction of the 1953 Transport Act gave the regions more independence. This Act abolished the Railway Executive, and gave overall control to the British Transport Commission under the chairmanship of Sir Brian Robertson. In 1956, the regions were allowed to introduce some of the old colour schemes on a number of main line express services. At this time, the general manager of the Western Region was K. W. C. Grand, and the chairman of the Western Region Board was R. F. Hanks, both were former Great Western men. The result was that WR wasted no time in revamping a number of its top services by repainting the BR Mk1 coaching stock in chocolate and cream livery. At the same time, a number of other services were named. The 'Bristolian' and the 'Merchant Venturer' served the Paddington to Bristol route. The 'Royal Duchy' and the 'Mayflower' ran to the South West. The long-running 'Cornish Riviera Express' also had a new headboard, and chocolate-and-cream coaches.

The 'Capitals United Express', the 'Red Dragon' and the 'Pembroke Coast Express' served South and West Wales. The 'Cheltenham Spa Express', although slower, brought back memories of the Great Western's pre-war 'Cheltenham Flyer'. One of the through services from

Below: **The biggest revolution to Western Region passenger services came with the arrival of the High Speed Trains (HSTs) during 1976/7. These new trains, which were capable of travelling at 125mph, completely transformed main line services on the Western Region in terms of both speed and comfort. In this view a power car from the Eastern Region unit No 254003 approaches Didcot on 5 November 1977 with the 9.08am service from Bristol Temple Meads to Paddington.** *Mark Yarwood/ Great Western Trust*

slightly less than 9mph! It is no wonder that some of this traffic was switched to road transport.

The Beeching cuts resulted in a large chunk of the Western Region's branch and secondary line system being closed to both passengers and freight. This effectively saw the end of the pick-up goods. The rundown and eventual withdrawal of steam traction in 1965, and the Clean Air Acts of 1956 and 1968, resulted in the reduction of domestic and industrial coal consumption and saw many of the South Wales pits close, with the knock-on effect of the closure of many of the lines that served them. In 1913, there were 600 rail-connected collieries in South Wales. In 1960, the South Wales collieries were producing some 12.5 million tons of coal, but by the 1980s, this had dropped to just over five million tons. Most of the remaining coal traffic on the Western comprised a much-reduced domestic coal service, which served a number of local distribution depots.

However, the large steelworks at Port Talbot and Llanwern were still at this time supplied from collieries in South Wales. Sadly, Tower Colliery at Hirwain which was the last deep pit colliery in Wales closed on 25 January 2008. Merry-go-round (MGR) trains comprising air-braked self-discharge wagons were first introduced in 1965, and were eventually used to supply the new power stations at Aberthaw on the Vale of Glamorgan line, and at Didcot, which from its opening in September 1970, was supplied by coal from the East Midlands pits.

One positive aspect of the Beeching report was that it freed up vital resources that were being bled away by unremunerative lines, and other antiquated working practices, this helped pave the way forward in the use of containerised air-braked block and company trains. The Freightliner train concept was introduced on the Western Region in 1967, with the first terminal opening at Pengam near Cardiff. From there, services were operated to Willesden, Sheffield, Liverpool, Manchester and Edinburgh. Another terminal was opened at Swansea in spring 1969, with services to the same locations, and also Harwich Parkstone Quay.

Under the 1968 Transport Act the Western Region liner trains were taken over, from 1 January 1969, by Freightliner Ltd, the company that still operates them today as part of the Freightliner Group. The introduction of these fast, long-distance air braked, block and company trains saw the rapid reduction in the use of older wagons, many of which dated from Great Western days.

In 1970, a rail connection was opened to Merehead Quarry in Somerset on the former Witham to Cheddar branch. The new block company aggregate trains were operated by Foster Yeoman, and served a number of railheads in the South East. Another company, Amey Roadstone, also started operating block aggregate trains from its quarry at Whatley on the old Frome to Radstock branch, the rail operations of the two concerns later being combined into Mendip Rail. (Amey sold their aggregate business to Hanson PLC in 1989.) In 1983, an international freight terminal was opened at Morris Cowley near Oxford, which was served daily by a container train from Harwich Parkstone Quay.

As mentioned previously, the end of the Western Region came on 10 June 1986 when the five remaining regions were abolished and replaced by new business sectors. The period between 1955 and 1986 had brought many changes on the Western Region, including the widespread closure of branch lines, the move from semaphore to multiple aspect signalling, electronic signalboxes, and the reconstruction of a number of stations. On the freight side, the period saw the complete removal of the pick-up goods, and the introduction of long-distance, air-braked, block and company trains.

One of the biggest changes during the period under review was the motive power: the removal of steam traction and its subsequent replacement with diesel-hydraulics, and then diesel-electrics, followed by the introduction of the HSTs. The 125mph HSTs brought a new era of high-speed travel, and by 1986, most of the main line services on the Western Region were operated with these trains, giving a fast, comfortable and reliable service that continues to this day.

During the early days of the Great Western Railway, Brunel wrote: 'I shall not attempt to argue with those who consider any increase of speed unnecessary. The public will always prefer that conveyance, which is the most perfect, and speed, within reasonable limits, is a material ingredient in perfection in travelling.' His words are as true today, as they were then.

Acknowledgements
I would like to thank the following for their help in producing this book: Hugh Ballantyne, David Holmes, Robin Isaac, Phillip Kelley, David Parker, Ray Viney, Ron White of Colour-Rail, and the Great Western Trust.

I
The 'Great Western' Region

Above: **For a number of years after Nationalisation, both services and infrastructure on BR Western Region remained virtually unchanged from Great Western Railway days. This can be seen to good effect in this picture of 'Castle' class No 5060 *Earl of Berkeley* from Old Oak Common (81A) as it approaches Banbury General in August 1956, with the 11.40am service from Birkenhead to Paddington. The train comprises a mixture of ex-Great Western and British Railways Mk1 stock in the early 'strawberry and cream' livery. In the far platform is a suburban set, including coach No W41047, built by BR at Swindon in July 1955 to a Great Western design.** *T. J. Edgington/Colour-Rail BRW 590*

Below: **Unlike today, when everyone seems to have a car, most holidaymakers in the 1950s travelled to the South West by train. During the holiday season through services, which were usually heavily loaded, ran to and from the South West from many parts of the country. Pictured here leaving Dawlish in July 1957, is the 1.25pm service from Paddington to Kingswear, hauled by ex-Great Western 'King' class 4-6-0 No 6009 *King Charles II* of Old Oak Common (81A).** *Peter Gray/Colour-Rail BRW 167*

Above: **Although ordered by the Great Western in 1946, the Brown Boveri A1A-A1A gas turbine locomotive No 18000 was not taken into service until 9 May 1950. It was purchased as an experimental locomotive, and was used on Western Region services until its withdrawal in December 1960. Nicknamed 'Kerosene Castle', it was not noted for its reliability, and was often out of service. It is pictured here at speed near Chippenham on a down Bristol express in 1956.**
P. M. Alexander/Colour-Rail DE 837

Right: **During the 1950s, the Western Region was still using motive power that had been designed and built back in the 19th century. One such class was the Dean Goods 0-6-0s, of which No 2516 was built at Swindon in March 1897, and is pictured here at Oswestry in 1952. It was withdrawn from service in May 1956, and is now on display at the Steam museum, Swindon. The last working member of the class, No 2538, was withdrawn from Oswestry (89A) a year later, in May 1957.**
P. B. Whitehouse/Colour-Rail BRW 635

Right: **One of the first major investments by British Railways was the introduction of twelve new Standard classes of locomotives for use on all regions. The 'Britannia' class Pacific 4-6-2s were designed at Derby in 1951 and introduced on Western Region services in 1952. Initially allocated to Old Oak Common and Plymouth Laira, they were used on services to the South West, but eventually, all 15 Western Region examples ended up at Cardiff Canton (86C) from where they saw extensive use on services between South Wales and Paddington, and over the North & West route to Shrewsbury. No 70028 *Royal Star*, in typical Cardiff Canton condition, stands at Cardiff General Station in July 1957.**
T.J. Edgington/Colour-Rail BRW 308

Above: **For the summer 1955 timetable, the Western Region introduced its first Pullman service, the 'South Wales Pullman'. This was a weekdays-only service that ran between Paddington and Swansea. The train first ran on 27 June 1955, and was primarily aimed at business travellers, departing from Paddington at 9.55am, returning to the Capital at 4.35pm. The down service is seen here near Wootton Bassett in the summer of 1960 hauled by 'Castle' class 4-6-0 No 7028 *Cadbury Castle* of Swansea Landore (87E).**
P. M. Alexander/
Colour-Rail BRW 1026

Right: **The up 'Red Dragon', the 7.30am service from Carmarthen to Paddington, headed by 'Castle' class No 5061 *Earl of Birkenhead,* speeds through Reading General in around 1961. This service was one of a number of named trains introduced by the Western Region during 1956.**
B. J. Swain/Colour-Rail BRW 402

Right: **The ex-Great Western Churchward-designed '2800/2884' class 2-8-0s were used by the Western Region on long-distance and heavy freight services, almost to the end of steam traction. No 2879 was built at Swindon in 1919, and is seen passing West Ealing with a down freight on 9 May 1962. This locomotive was withdrawn in August 1964, but more than 30 members of the class were still working in 1965.**
Charles Gordon-Stuart/
Great Western Trust

Above: The end of an era, as a slip coach, one of three converted from Hawksworth brake composites in 1958, arrives at Bicester in May 1960. It had been slipped from the rear of the 5.10pm fast service from Paddington to Wolverhampton, and would then have been attached to the 4.34pm Paddington to Wolverhampton stopping service. The Bicester slip was the last such working in the country, the final occasion being made from the same service on 9 September 1960.
J. Mullett/Colour-Rail BRW 328

Below: The Western Region inherited 37 diesel railcars from the Great Western Railway. Apart from a few early withdrawals, the WR continued to use a number of these vehicles right up until the early 1960s. Pictured here at Ledbury in May 1959, as the driver exchanges tokens with the signalman, is No W19 of Gloucester (85B), built at Swindon in 1940. It is painted in the BR strawberry and cream livery.
R. E. Toop/Colour-Rail DE 703

Top: **This picture was also taken at Ledbury, on a frosty 24 December 1962, and shows ex-Great Western 2-6-2T No 5152 (minus smokebox numberplate) arriving with the four-coach Hereford portion of the 9.15am service from Paddington to Worcester and Hereford.**
P. A. Fry/Great Western Trust

Above: **'Hall' class 4-6-0 No 6957 *Norcliffe Hall* of Bristol Bath Road (82A), heads a down service to Worcester and Hereford past Shottesbrooke, Berkshire on 4 August 1959. The front two coaches are still in the early BR strawberry and cream livery, the rest are in the later standard BR maroon livery.** *Mark Yarwood/Great Western Trust*

Left: 'Manor' class 4-6-0 No 7829 *Ramsbury Manor* stands at Carmarthen Town on 12 June 1963 with a service from Pembroke Dock to Paddington. Interestingly, the service reversed here, and again at Swansea. The 'Manors' were ideal locomotives for this type of working with a number ending up on the Cambrian lines in North Wales. No 7829 was built by BR Western Region at Swindon in December 1950, the last of the class to be constructed. *Charles Gordon-Stuart/ Great Western Trust*

Below left: In 1959, a start was made on electrifying the route between Euston and Wolverhampton, and it was at this time that a one-hour interval service was introduced between Paddington, Birmingham and Wolverhampton Low Level. To operate these trains the majority of the 'King' class 4-6-0s were allocated to Old Oak Common and Wolverhampton Stafford Road. On 19 May 1962, No 6017 *King Edward IV* passes a rather run down Aynho Park Halt with the 7.40am service from Birkenhead to Paddington. The halt, which was situated on the high level line at Aynho, was closed on 7 January 1963. *P. A. Fry/ Great Western Trust*

Below: Inter-regional cross-country services formed an important part of the timetable. Many were summer-only trains, but the Bournemouth West to Newcastle service ran throughout the year. Seen here at Banbury on 14 May 1962, is 'Modified Hall' class 4-6-0 No 7905 *Fowey Hall* of Banbury (84C), on the 8.35am from Newcastle to Bournemouth West. The first vehicle is an ex-Southern Railway four-wheel horse van. Banbury was the first major station to be completely rebuilt under the 1955 Modernisation Plan. Work was started in removing the old station in 1956 and it was completed in 1958. *Charles Gordon-Stuart/ Great Western Trust*

Above: **The 'County' class were the most powerful two-cylinder 4-6-0s on the Western Region. They were used on a variety of services ranging from express passenger to parcels and freight. They produced some of their best work on services in Devon and Cornwall and here, climbing Dainton Bank on 5 August 1961 with the 9.5am service from Birkenhead to Plymouth, comprising mostly London Midland Region coaching stock, is No 1005 *County of Devon* of Bristol Bath Road (82A).** *Hugh Ballantyne*

Below: **Another inter-regional cross-country service, the 12.56pm service from Cardiff to Brighton, hauled by Cardiff Canton (86C)-allocated No 5097 *Sarum Castle*, speeds through Freshford station on 21 April 1962. This route, which runs via Bath and Salisbury, still forms an important part of the cross-country network.**
P. A. Fry/Great Western Trust

Above: **The 'Grange' class were probably the best of the mixed traffic 4-6-0s and many survived until the end of steam, but none into preservation. Passing through Newport on 21 November 1964, with a down Class D fully fitted express freight, is No 6859 *Yiewsley Grange* of Cardiff East Dock (88A). It was withdrawn on 18 November 1965.** *P. A. Fry/Great Western Trust*

Below: **Class 1400 0-4-2T No 1450, together with two six-wheel milk tank wagons, stands at Hemyock on 28 August 1964. The line was closed to passenger traffic on 9 September 1963, but remained open to serve the St Ivel creamery and was finally closed on 31 October 1975.** *Mark Yarwood/Great Western Trust*

Above: **An up pick-up goods waits under the overall roof at Tavistock South station on 16 June 1962, hauled by Plymouth Laira (83D)-based '4575' class 2-6-2T No 5541. Tavistock was situated on the Plymouth to Launceston branch, which was closed to passenger traffic on 31 December 1962, but remained open for freight until 7 September 1964.** *P. A. Fry/Great Western Trust*

Below: **Class 5700 0-6-0PT No 9676 banked by another member of the class, approaches Cefn Coed on the single-track Pontsticill Loop with the 9.30am aggregate train from Vaynor Quarry to Merthyr, on 19 October 1963. This former Brecon & Merthyr/London & North Western joint line was closed on 4 May 1964.** *P. A. Fry/Great Western Trust*

Top: **By the early 1960s, many of the 'Castles' that had been displaced from passenger services by the diesel-hydraulics were to be found on secondary duties including freights. Passing West Ealing station on 14 February 1962, is No 7034** *Ince Castle* **on a down milk service from Kensington to the South West. With increasing amounts being moved by road, milk trains from the South West to West Ealing and Kensington were withdrawn by the Western Region in the early 1970s.**
Charles Gordon-Stuart/Great Western Trust

Above: **Bulk oil trains formed an important part of freight traffic on the Western Region. Here BR Standard Class 9F No 92218 of Southall (81C), passes Patchway with a down oil train on 29 February 1964. The '9Fs' were probably the best of the BR Standard classes, with the WR operating over 40 examples.** *P. A. Fry/Great Western Trust*

4
Steam Depots

Above: **A feature of the days of steam traction were the motive power depots (MPDs), or locomotive sheds. One of the delights during the 1950s and '60s was visiting these 'temples of steam'. The depots ranged from the small, single-road engine shed, to the largest on the WR at Old Oak Common (81A). The end of steam traction saw the majority closed, but a few remained open as diesel depots and stabling points. On 1 January 1960 81A had an allocation of 192 locomotives of which 167 were steam, with a large number of 'King', 'Castle' and 'Hall' class 4-6-0s. Seen here, in September 1955, inside the main shed which contained four turntables, is one of last remaining 'Star' class 4-6-0s, No 4061** *Glastonbury Abbey* **of Wolverhampton Stafford Road (84A). Old Oak Common was opened by the Great Western Railway on 17-March 1906 and was closed to steam by the WR on 22 March 1965.** *T. B. Owen/Colour-Rail BRW 414*

Below: **Bristol Bath Road (82A) was another large steam shed. The Bristol & Exeter Railway had opened a locomotive shed on this site in 1850, but the main building seen here was opened by the Great Western in 1934. Waiting to leave the shed yard in June 1959 is a 'Castle' class 4-6-0, fully cleaned and serviced ready to work the up 'Bristolian' service to London. Bath Road was closed to steam during 1961, re-opening as a diesel depot on 18 June 1962, and closed completely in June 1995.** *Colour-Rail BRW 532*

Above: **In this picture, taken at Plymouth Laira on 29 April 1962, 'Castle' No 7022** *Hereford Castle,* **and 'Grange' No 6863** *Dolhywel Grange,* **stand in the shed yard. Alongside the locomotives is one of the water cranes, and underneath a 'fire devil' used in the winter to stop the water freezing. At this date, Laira had been converted to service the new diesel-hydraulic fleet, and behind the water crane is a fuel oil dispenser. Opened by the Great Western in 1901, it was closed to steam in April 1964. The site is now covered by Laira HST depot.** *Charles Gordon-Stuart/ Great Western Trust*

Left: **Class 2251 0-6-0 No 2241 of Hereford (86C), receives attention at Gloucester MPD on 13 April 1962. Behind the locomotive is the 65ft turntable, shed building and water tower. Gloucester was opened by the Great Western in 1854 and was enlarged in 1872. It remained open until the end of steam, closing on 31 December 1965.** *Charles Gordon-Stuart/ Great Western Trust*

43

Left: **The coaling and ash disposal road at Severn Tunnel Junction shed, on 25 June 1963. In the foreground of the row of eight locomotives is '2884' class 2-8-0 No 3844 of Pontypool Road (86G). Severn Tunnel Junction (86E) was opened by the Great Western in 1907 and closed in October 1965.**
Charles Gordon-Stuart/ Great Western Trust

Left: **Standing in the yard at Swindon shed (82C) on 1 December 1963, and minus its smokebox numberplate, is a rather rundown looking 'County' class 4-6-0, No 1014** *County of Glamorgan.*
It was withdrawn just five months later, on 24 April 1964. The shed building seen here was opened in 1908, and as this picture shows, had seen better days; it was closed on 31 October 1964. The Great Western Society is currently building a replica *County of Glamorgan* **at the Didcot Railway Centre.**
Charles Gordon-Stuart/ Great Western Trust

Above: **Although under London Midland Region control, some services on the Cambrian were operated by 'Manor' class 4-6-0s until 1965. Here, climbing Bow Street bank on 6 August 1965, is No 7822 *Foxcote Manor* of Machynlleth (6F), on the up 'Cambrian Coast Express', the 09.45 service from Aberystwyth to Paddington. Withdrawn from service in November 1965, *Foxcote Manor* is now preserved on the Llangollen Railway.** *P. A. Fry/Great Western Trust*

Below: **For many years after the end of main line steam traction, the only steam-operated service on BR was the 1ft 11½in gauge Vale of Rheidol Railway which runs between Aberystwyth and Devil's Bridge. The line passed to London Midland Region control on 1 January 1963, but for a few years at least, the locomotives were still turned out in BR Western Region green. At Nantyronen Halt on 22 August 1966, No 7 *Owain Glyndŵr* hauls the 14.45 service from Aberystwyth. The whole line was sold to the Brecon Mountain Railway Company on 31 March 1989.** *Great Western Trust*

7
Diesel Multiple-Units

Above: **On 12 September 1960, the Western Region introduced three new eight-car air-conditioned Blue Pullman trains. Built by Metro-Cammell they were used on services from London Paddington to Birmingham and Wolverhampton, Bristol, and South Wales. On 11 February 1964 No W60099 in the distinctive blue and white Pullman livery, passes West Ealing at the head of the down 'Bristol Pullman', the 12.45 service from Paddington.**
Charles Gordon-Stuart/ Great Western Trust

Left: **Standing at Bath Spa on the 16 April 1973 is a former Blue Pullman set on the down service from Paddington to Bristol. During 1966, all three sets were repainted in the later BR blue and grey livery with yellow ends, as seen here. These distinctive trains were withdrawn from service on 4 May 1973.**
Hugh Ballantyne

Right: **The Derby-built Class 116 three-car suburban diesel multiple-units were introduced by the Western Region on services between Cardiff and Treherbert from 11 September 1957. DMU services were extended to cover all of the Valley lines on 13 January 1958. Seen arriving at Radyr in around 1959 is a pair of Class 116 units with a service from Treherbert to Barry Island.**
Great Western Trust

Right: **The Western Region ordered a number of Class 117 three-car units from the Pressed Steel Company in 1959 for use on the London suburban services. Standing at Ealing Broadway on 17 March 1962, with an up stopping service, is a three-car set with No W51332 leading. The unit is in green with a grey cab top, route numbers and yellow 'V' cat's whiskers warning stripes. By the mid-1960s a number of these units were also operating from Bristol, Cardiff and Plymouth. The '117s' gave tremendous service on Thames Valley services for over 30 years, until being replaced by the Class 165 Turbos in 1993.**
Charles Gordon-Stuart/ Great Western Trust

Right: **A Swindon-built Class 120 three-car cross-country set is pictured at St Dennis Junction on 17 June 1962 with the 9.53am service from Newquay to Par. This is one of the second batch of Class 120 three-car units that were built at Swindon in 1961.** *P.A. Fry/ Great Western Trust*

59

Left: **The Western Region took delivery of 20 Gloucester RCW-built Class 122 single-car units during 1959. These were for use on branch lines, many of which had been previously operated by auto train push-pull services. Standing in the branch platform at Wellington (Salop) on 18 July 1962, with a service to Much Wenlock, is No W55009. The Much Wenlock branch was closed to passengers on 23 July 1962.**
Charles Gordon-Stuart/
Great Western Trust

Below left: **In 1960, the Western ordered a further 15 Class 121 single-car units from Pressed Steel. Standing at the single platform at Abingdon on 27 March 1962 is No W55031 with an afternoon service to Radley. The introduction of these units on many Western Region branch services did not, as anticipated, stem the losses, and only extended the closure date for many lines by a few years. Apart from the conversion from gas to electric lighting, Abingdon had probably seen little investment since it was re-constructed in 1908. The branch was closed to passengers on 9 September 1963, and to freight on 30 June 1984.** *P. A. Fry/*
Great Western Trust

Below: **This view of Class 122 single-car No W55003 at Bromyard on 28 November 1963 is included as it shows the rundown state of the station. This was typical at this time on many branch and secondary lines that had been earmarked for closure. Bromyard was on the Worcester to Leominster line, from which passenger services were withdrawn on 7 September 1964.**
Charles Gordon-Stuart/
Great Western Trust

Above: The use of four-wheel railbuses on some branch lines did not work either, only delaying closure for a few years. The lack of passengers is quite evident in this picture of AC Cars No W79978 as it waits at Tetbury on 30 March 1964, with the 17.58 service to Kemble. The branch was closed to passengers on 6 April 1964. No W79978 is now preserved on the Colne Valley Railway.
P. A. Fry/
Great Western Trust

Left: The line from West Drayton to Uxbridge Vine Street was opened by the Great Western on 8 September 1856, and was the first of the Thames Valley branches to be closed to passenger traffic by the Western Region. The terminus station at Vine Street is seen here on 8 September 1962, the last day of passenger services. Arriving from Paddington is a three-car Class 117 DMU headed by No W51360.
Charles Gordon-Stuart
Great Western Trust

Right: **Between 1957 and 1961 some 147 D2000 series, (later Class 03) diesel-mechanical shunting locomotives were built at Swindon. These 204hp 0-6-0s were used on both the Western and other regions. Standing in the works yard at Swindon on 9 April 1961 are Nos D2143 and D2145, both having been completed just a few weeks previously.**
Charles Gordon-Stuart/ Great Western Trust

Below right: **The '03s' were generally used on short freight and shunting turns, but this picture shows No D2195 together with ex-Great Western 'B' set coaches Nos W6831 and W1238 at Highworth on 18 June 1962, with an unadvertised workmen's train from Swindon. The branch was actually closed to passenger traffic on 2 March 1953, but remained open for freight traffic, and apart from a short section at the Swindon end, was closed completely on 6 August 1962.**
Hugh Ballantyne

Below: **An interesting working in West Wales shows Class 03s Nos 03119, 03141 and 03142 from Landore approaching Pembury near Burry Port on 7 September 1983, with a coal train from Cwm Mawr on the Burry Port & Gwendraeth Valley line. This route has a number of low bridges so the '03s' were ideal when fitted with cut-down cabs. However, they were withdrawn in February 1986, and from that date until June 1987, the branch was worked using three reduced-height Class 08 shunters. The line is currently disused.** *Hugh Ballantyne*

9
The Diesel-Electric Era

Above: **The introduction of diesel-electric locomotives on the Western Region started with the delivery of the first of the English Electric Type 3s (later Class 37) in March 1963. No D6841 was delivered new to Cardiff Canton in May 1963, and is seen here at Severn Tunnel Junction on 25 June 1963. These locomotives took over many of the freight services in South Wales.** *Charles Gordon-Stuart/Great Western Trust*

Right: **The steam depot at Newport Ebbw Junction was closed in October 1965 and was replaced by a new, standard BR-pattern diesel servicing depot, which was situated alongside the South Wales main line. The depot is seen here on 13 June 1971, and standing outside are a couple of Brush Type 4s, far left, English Electric Type 3 No D6939, BR 'Peak' Type 4 No D154, right, and '08' No D4014 inside.** *Hugh Ballantyne*

Above: **Class 37 No 37257 on down coal empties passes Pengam Freightliner terminal Cardiff on 13 September 1979. Pengam was opened in June 1967 by the then Minister of Transport Barbara Castle, and was the first purpose-built Freightliner terminal on the Western Region.** *Hugh Ballantyne*

Below: **A scenic view of Newport Ebbw Junction on 13 September 1979 as Class 37 No 37176 on a short freight, passes another member of the class waiting in the sidings. The line off to the left runs to Park Junction and the freight-only branches to Machen and Ebbw Vale.** *Hugh Ballantyne*

Top: A pair of Class 37s, Nos 37231 and 37213, both allocated to Cardiff Canton (CF) stand at the stabling point at Llantrisant on 6 July 1985. This small stabling point was situated in part of the old goods shed, and is typical of a number of diesel stabling points on the Western Region at that time. *David Parker*

Above: St Blazey was one steam depot that remained open as a diesel depot long after the end of steam traction. Standing in the yard in July 1983 are, from left to right: Class 37 No 37185, Class 08 No 08945 and Class 37 No 37205. At the time of writing, St Blazey is still operational, but the original Cornwall Minerals Railway half roundhouse building, which dates from around 1872, is in industrial use. *David Parker*

Above: **To celebrate the 150th anniversary of the Great Western Railway in 1985, the Western Region painted a Class 117 suburban DMU in chocolate and cream livery. The set, No B430, comprising Nos 51368, 59520 and 51410, is seen here in the West Midland sidings at Oxford in June 1985.** *David Parker*

Below: **During 1985, a number of Leyland Class 142 railbuses were allocated to Plymouth Laira for use on some of the remaining Cornish branch lines. Seen here at Roche on a service to Newquay on 30 June 1986 is set No 142023 in chocolate and cream livery. The '142s', which were known as 'Skippers' on the Western Region, were unsuccessful in Cornwall due mainly to excessive flange wear that was caused by the tight curves on some of the branch lines, but nevertheless, they returned in 2008 for use by First Great Western.** *David Parker*

10
Swindon Finale

Right: **With the withdrawal of the remaining 'Western' class diesel-hydraulics in 1976, locomotive repairs at Swindon diminished, and by the early 1980s the works was repairing '08' shunters and DMUs. During its final years, Swindon Works became a dump for withdrawn diesel-electric locomotives as can be seen in this picture taken on 11 April 1984. In view are nine Class 08s and three Class 25s, all awaiting the torch. At this time the works yard was awash with withdrawn locomotives.** *Author*

Left: **This view of the weighshop at Swindon was taken on 22 March 1984. Standing in the building is a withdrawn ex-London Midland Region 'Peak' Class 46 No 46044, outside is newly refurbished '08' shunter No 08693, and on the right, another '08', No 08604. Over 400 diesel-electric locomotives were cut up at Swindon, including 47 'Peaks'. The weighshop still stands today, and is part of a local brewery.** *Author*

Right: **Part of the works at Swindon continued to repair DMUs right up until closure. Under repair on 3 December 1985 is Southern Region Class 205 DEMU set No 1130, and a Western Region Class 122 single-car unit. The whole of the works was closed in 1986 with the site being sold to Tarmac Properties. Much of the site is now covered with housing, but some of the old works buildings have seen further use as a retail outlet centre, and the Steam museum. The old works drawing office now houses the National Monuments Record Office.** *David Parker*